The Simple Changes

Poems by
Stuart P. Radowitz

San Francisco | Fairfield | Delhi

The Simple Changes

Copyright ©2024 by Stuart P. Radowitz

All rights reserved. Printed in the United States of America. No part of this book may be used or reproduced in any manner whatsoever without written permission except in the case of brief quotations embodied in critical articles and reviews. For information contact:

Blue Light Press
www.bluelightpress.com
Email: bluelightpress@aol.com

1st World Library
PO Box 2211
Fairfield, Iowa 52556
www.1stworldpublishing.com

Cover Artwork: Prartho Sereno

Author Photo: Dr. Sherry Radowitz

First Edition

ISBN: 978-1-4218-3564-8

Library of Congress Cataloging-in-Publication Data

For Jesse, and my brother Andrew
and Stephanie, Dave, Emily, Ryan, mom and dad,
and, of course, Gigi

Wind

I have come
to the bottom
of my soul.

Too much wind!

Acknowledgments

For Gabriella Laskaris, with much love and thanks for her advice and assistance in the preparation of this book.

A special thank you to Prartho Sereno, for both her beautiful cover art and her inspiration.

For Diane, with love and gratitude.

Some of these poems first appeared in: *Aspen Leaves: A Literary Magazine* (Aspen Magazine); *The Avocet: A Journal of Nature Poetry* (Charles Portolano); *Bards Annual 2019* (Local Gems Press); *Fragments: A Literary Review* (Seattle University); *Nassau County Poet Laureate Society Review: 2022, 2023* (Nassau County Poet Laureate Society); *Nassau County Voices in Verse: 2020, 2022, 2023* (Local Gems Press); *Pandemic Puzzle Poems* (Blue Light Press); *Poetry in the Plaza: Village of Great Neck Plaza* (online); *PPA Literary Review: Volume 24* (Performance Poets Association).

The poem, "Closer to God," was read at the Bethany French Baptist Church, Jamaica, N.Y. in celebration of Dr. Martin Luther King Jr. Day, Monday, January 16, 2017.

Contents

House Plants 1
After Lorca 2
A Gentle Unraveling 3
On the Ferry to Groton 4
Man is Found Wanting, Again 5
Apart 6
In Late Night 7
After the Sound 8
Movement 9
Hawks 10
The Moon Casts a Light 11
Life Unleashed 12
Blueberries 13
Right Here in River City 14
Wrong Choices 15
While You Were Away 16
When You Give Your Love Away 17
Anticipating Renewal 18
Listen Closely 19
Seven Mornings 20
Unknowing 21
Maui Mountain 22
Landscaping the Mind, Transforming the Innocent 23
The Everywhere Spirit 24
Gracious Space Sacred Place 25
In Deep Wood 26

Looking Through a Window Into Someone Else's Life 27
A Moment in Time.................................... 28
Looking at the Power of God Through the Eyes of a Man.. 29
Transparent.. 30
Amsterdam Delft Blue................................. 31
Learning to Exhale 32
Alone 33
A Safe Place to Rest................................... 34
Obsession 35
All Sense of the Future is Lost 36
Living at Sea Level.................................... 37
Morning 38
The Wind is Music 39
Sky Flashed with Light 40
Northern Hotel....................................... 41
A Light Wind 42
A Previous Life 43
The Simple Changes.................................. 44
November.. 45
Fall 46
Balance 47
Water 48
Just Someone I Used to Know.......................... 49
The Morning Star 50
Closer to God 51
Living Beyond My Means 52
The Chamber of Light 53

About the Author 54

House Plants

Those who are the most kind
change into flowers
or garden plants.

Your whole soul rests
in a single flower.
The blossoms and seeds

are yours forever.
Perfection sleeps in your roots
and can never be cut.

After Lorca

Forest stands out back and is lit
by piles of starfish and burning wood.

Sun and moon link arms.
Orange of the meadow, fish of the sea

join in a slow dance to the city.
Sky crawls on building ledges waiting

for last rituals to begin.
Tonight, worms and lizards mourn.

A Gentle Unraveling

Three moons
November North Star
tangerine orange glow.

Cheyenne to Fort Collins
a half hour drive,
long stretches of dry grass.

Stuck in off-road mud under green pine.
Time is not a priority but a gift from within.
Relationships revolve at dizzying speeds.

Copper pots hang on the wall.
When you give yourself to another
you don't know if or when it will end.

All my possessions have disappeared.
Books, art, cars, home gone.
Snowy egrets, Canada geese, three fish hawks circle.

The totality of all the spirits you love
and that love you, push you through this planet.
Strands of my life whipped by wind.

On the Ferry to Groton

Sometimes
I like to think of you
cooking, in the kitchen, kids
coming and going, asking questions
doing homework, stirring a skillet.

Doors open and shut,
darkness comes and goes, music recedes.
On the ferry to Groton I see osprey,
your eyes wide rays of light,
windows to the soul.

Man is Found Wanting, Again

The moon is not right tonight,
not perfect enough.

Like the face of a man
who has lost his child.

We fly into a blinding light.

Apart

Tonight
our bodies have come
and fall away.

Our faces have joined
and separate
like clouds in a near sky.

The moments of calm pass.
There is no end
to our being apart.

In Late Night

In late night
air is moonlit and faces
seem to be in the fields.

Close to the ground I listen.
There is nothing
but the slash of weather.

The pond reeds are still
as the dark recedes.
Beyond the drift snow, morning comes.

After the Sound

After the sound
the parting of space begins.

Stones, and leaves of water
form the separation of places.

Four days of rain
have pushed flat all contour.

Breathless, motions cease.
This is the departing.

Movement

The day has passed.
I have come to be still.

The day has passed in movement
that has come to be still.

Around the day I have passed
watching the signs of movement.

The signs are movement.
If we are still, the signs pass.

Hawks

Still snow surrounds the house.
Absolute white settles
around my body.

The winter hawks
live on nothing, glowing
like shadows of light.

Day after day they circle,
silent and dark as air.

They are furious hawks, my brothers,
safe as cold moons,
willing to eat eyes.

The Moon Casts a Light

The moon casts a light
over the face of everyone.
Night is deeper than ever.
Nothing like a breeze blows.

I watch the moon change,
slowly thickening
until every inch of air is gone.
Sun leaves the air dry.

The moon fades.
It is any other day.
The earth is our mirror.
Our deaths last forever.

Life Unleashed

In deep willow valley
willows six feet tall surround us.
Distant ocean barely seen.

I don't think about you
as often as I used to
but I still do.

I saw a flower born this morning.
In the afternoon our world changed.
So many branches have been cut or withered.

Down the Carmel coast basking seals.
Predators lie out of view.
Dark night covers the shoreline.

Blueberries

In the end
it must all come
to this.

A blue heron,
a back trail
leading in,

wet marshlands,
picked
blueberries.

Right Here in River City

Fruit laden and foul - Pablo Neruda

In July or August
or whenever it is that
fresh summer fruit ripens,

I undress your flowers
pull your hands up over your head
and untie your jewels.

Wrong Choices

I guess I can drink coffee until the end
depending on how I go.
Darkness wraps around my heart like fat.

Days without direction, wrong choices
bring me, us, to the edge again.

I take comfort in the yards of topsoil
placed on my tomato bed.

When I die the bird spirit will come
and fly my soul away.
I will see my brother and son and speak to both.

I will speak to all my grandparents, mother and father.
After I visit with my daughter and her children,
I will be gone.

While You Were Away

While you were away
I rode a bike, called a friend,
had lunch at The River Café.
Picked up pine cones from the deck.
Put them in a basket to save.

Pine trees and broken dirt
split earth and chewed up grass.
The lusciousness of a primordial forest,
sensuous winds.
Before you came back I met someone else.
She was that forest, all ancient and new growth together.

A warm mid-March sun.
A change in direction, new people new places.
Sunlight streaming through an upstairs window.

When You Give Your Love Away

The lightest wind, breeze, breath
brings me to your side.
Picture a cypress tree, green moss hanging.
I need to see you tonight.

Instead I see three moons over a valley
snow on a wagon, tarot cards.
When we miss someone
it goes on long after death.

A friendly spirit or loved one might look down,
take an interest in your well-being.
A man walking to temple might say hello.
When you give your love away, does it come back?

Anticipating Renewal

Oh, it's the hunger.
Looking back at a picture of you and him
from forty years ago,
I notice your nails are red.
A small detail overlooked.
Beneath the surface, hard sharp edges.

In a used car and scrap metal junkyard
in Canarsie, Brooklyn, a chop shop.
An old junkyard dog lays in the mud and oil.

He has been used, abused, chased,
hit with rocks and sticks,
so he can be mean.

They leave him out in the weather at night.
A watchdog to protect the yard,
scare off kids and thieves.
I can feel headwinds in my heart.
The hunger never stops.

Listen Closely

Light shines on lovers.
It is one person opening their heart
and then both.
He wore the blue flannel shirt
and gave it to you or you took it
as a symbol of love.
Wear this. Keep warm. Feel me near you.

Listen closely to the whisper of the wind.
Sins of our parents follow us.
Ghosts are always here.
As I listen to the big jets fly overhead,
a gaping wound opens.
Pieces of my heart tumble out.

Seven Mornings
        endangered species

For three weeks
I have eaten nothing
but rice and potatoes.

I begin to hallucinate
visions of the world.

Last night I dreamt
five bears were shot
in a frame house.

They were lying on their backs
still breathing when I came in.
I climbed up a ladder

to the second floor.
They had huge heads
and pot bellies.

I felt strange
because they were dying and
there are so few bears left alive.
Then I saw the lake
split into seven mornings,
a brown bear cub, drinking.

Unknowing

Stepping into the abyss
I see the forest resetting.
A washed-out stream bed holds no water.

Secrets of our parents follow us.
Everything is magic. Frozen air
out of sync.

Gone off the earth, of the earth but gone.
The already dead know nothing of this
or knowing, are not concerned.

A ladybug lands on my arm.
A few minutes later another one
on my hand.

When my three-year old granddaughter Emily
holds her hand over my coffee cup,
she says *steam* and smiles.

Distant faces speak to me.
My grandmothers Eleanor and Rebecca,
grandfathers Abraham and Solomon.

I become a bridge for others to cross
a portal to enter, soft rolling hills.
Everything changes again.

Maui Mountain

(before the fire)

Friday the twenty-seventh.
10 a.m. raining in Maui.
Finally, a cleansing rain.

In Colorado I was a construction worker framing houses.
On cold snowy mornings I didn't want to work.
I would go to a little coffee shop, the Rainbow Café
drink coffee, try to stay warm and write.

Running on the beach, black volcanic sand
your spirit far away.
There is something about moving on in life,
changing direction, listening
to my neighbor's wind chimes.

I take meaning from the thirteenth full moon.
A star of Bethlehem moon.
Deepest buried thoughts surface.
The teeth of a dragon, touch of a butterfly.

Listening to the sound of the wind,
lime green birds in the cedar.
It's like freebasing life,
boiling it down, distilling words until
they become rain on the slopes of Maui Mountain.

Landscaping the Mind, Transforming the Innocent

Like vapors that disappear in clear cold air
damaged souls not fixable,
Dante's circle already assigned.

It's the way I say it that makes it sound bad.
The Marlboro Man dying of cancer.
Friends the same.

But things pivot. Babies are born
vaccines invented.
It gives us reason for hope.

Scattered fragments, broken urns,
original sin still prevails.
Above, celestial beings observe us all.

The Everywhere Spirit
for my father

Immortal sky
stars, soul
all the dead are
in your eyes.

Lost soul
wandering the street of generations.
When I'm here
cactus are tall, green, straight.

When I'm there –
(there)
it is always
your eyes, your eyes.

Gracious Space Sacred Place

In the hour of darkness everything is turmoil.
All is cool, gray, windy.
I look into my face in the mirror.
Aging, stillness of time.
I changed my side of the bed
feeling you, where you used to lay.

Neighbors eat dinner.
I never had the need for anyone but you
until now. Behind you
light blue sky, wispy white clouds,
stark green cedar.

In Deep Wood

In the deep wood darkness is slow
and never really over.

In the window of an Indian gift shop
Edward S. Curtis photographs circa 1889-1890.

A man, his hands thick like the hands of a farmer,
another man's hands.

In pale light I saw the shadow of a bird
through closed eyes.

The moon hangs in the sky and has broken into
a thousand little moons.

Looking Through a Window
Into Someone Else's Life

It's a very bitter day.
If you pass away on a bright sunny day,
it would be a good day
to enter the hearts of those you love.

If you pass away tomorrow on a cloudy rainy day,
it would be a good day
to become spirit and soul
and enter the hearts of those you love.

Time has no meaning.
Roots of my biggest pine
rise up through the earth like fingers
reaching to pull you back.

A Moment in Time

People orbit around me.
Thin cold air, a few stars,
a fine line.

When you become spirit
time freezes, ceases to exist.

Driving cross country big rig trucks
stay on course, in lane, steady.

Fluid air shimmers on the interstate.
Crossing over should be simple.

If you go too far,
there is no coming back.

Looking at the Power of God Through the Eyes of a Man

Half-moon in early evening,
still light, a shower of stars.
Take a step back.
A fragile balance between us.
We spend time together on the deck,
go our separate ways.
Island Park, down by the water
erosion erases the past.
Looking into your eyes,
years stretch ahead, minutes pass.
Your face changes. Now
it sounds like announcements
at a train station.
Time is garbled, slides by
as the station master advises,
your soul takes its own journey,
alone, while you are alive.
Afterwards the crossover is easier.

Transparent

In the garden of Emily Dickinson
must rest a bird or squirrel.
Cherry tomatoes grow on my deck.
When I see a reflection of myself
it is someone else.

In every house there are certain doors
I will not go behind.
I choose to remain here.
A blue mountain lake.
No doors, only mirrors.

Amsterdam Delft Blue

Flowery language is gone.
I tell everyone bad news, hard things.
The Flower of Babylon has closed.
We all suffer.
Bent over, humbling, forever in genuflection.
Others do penance for long ago transgressions.

In the garden dark shades of green.
A canopy of cedar, blue spruce, and white pine.
I keep hearing my name called,
softly, faintly.
Is it one of Dante's Circles calling
or my mother saying hello?

Learning to Exhale

The creek bed behind my house
has run dry.
Windy days blow away lies.
Coffee cups measure time.
Wind howling in the trees
sounds like waves on the ocean.

The forest floor is littered
with dried leaves, branch debris, scat.
Little bones from the eaten.
Ancient tales of burial.
In my backyard I too have buried animals:
birds, a squirrel, our bunny Pebbles, Misty the cat.

Where do I see beauty now?
Still clouds, sky—
air, clean and pure.

Alone

Look at this light shining in.
My heart opened itself to this for you.
The glare is like a four-sided mirror surrounding us.

When I opened the door,
I startled a blue jay a foot from my face.
Startling discoveries, clarity of vision, tonight's full moon.

This moon shatters and shadows us.
The sound of wind in my son's empty bedroom,
countless souls living in the gusts.

A thousand grains of sand,
millions of pine needles.
You and I, each of us alone.

A Safe Place to Rest

My son is standing in the bedroom doorway
looking at his mother.
She always sees him this way.

If there is any lesson in this,
breathe deeply, stay centered.
Listen to Lucinda Williams singing *Magnolia*.

Pause, read a nature poem.
Pause, write a nature poem.
Stay centered. Find a safe place to rest.

Obsession

Each fall, when you leave
I bring in the plants
that have survived.

I look at the ocean at night,
darkness and crashing waves.
The whales and elephants are leading.
What are they telling us? Should we follow?

Camping at Lake George in a borrowed tent,
not waterproof and then a deluge.
We threw everything into the car
especially ourselves, and headed off.

I commissioned two paintings.
A watercolor of our house by Natalie Katz,
an artist in Rockville Centre.
A painting of Snuffy, our giant tortoise,
by Prartho Sereno, a Marin County artist and poet.

Now that both are finished and framed,
I turn my attention outside.
The eternal flame burns brightly
but I can only see it
from the corner of my eye
as shadows pass briefly by.

Iron and steel and gossamer thread –
it's hard not to think about being dead.
Late at night lying in bed
stare into the dark, it's all in my head.

All Sense of the Future is Lost

Sunlight is brilliant this morning, shimmering.
For ten years I drove to the cemetery every week.
Now I am more casual about it.

For eleven years, almost twelve,
you have been gone. Even in grief
peaceful days come.

Your fate was not to live a long life.
Yours was intensity, maximum
movement, streams of friends.

When my son passed away, it was at home
in his own bed, mom and dad nearby
unable to save him.

When my brother passed away
it was ten thousand miles from home
alone, laying on a cold kitchen floor.

Listening to the wind and the cars
on the overpass, I am reminded
our time here is not forever.

This morning a bird lay dead
under my tallest pine,
her head bitten off.

Everyone writes their own book of life.

Living at Sea Level

A barely visible white half-moon,
blue sky, a face of many layers.
Evergreens are all I see.
Beyond the pines are wetlands,
orange brown shrub low to the ground.

This morning, when I opened the front door
a bird flew past me down the hall
straight into the back door.
Stunned she dropped
landing on a towel on the floor.

I picked the towel up
and carried her out back.
She lay unmoving for twenty minutes,
then up on her feet. I took some pictures
as the young cardinal flew away.

Later in the day I heard a thud.
Another bird had crashed my back window.
She lay dead.
When I looked closely, it was the same bird.
I buried her deep, back of my garden.

Shimmering air wavers, bodies reduced to dust.
Portals open. The moon bleeds into the sky.
Sometimes birds come to me to die.
They know I will bury them carefully,
look after their spirit.

Eventually we all get split up,
go our own way. In the afterlife
our interactions are less frequent,
more of our own path with occasional interruptions.
Sometimes, I see the bird spirit at the cemetery.

Morning

Morning sunlight glints off clouds,
sand, your hair, my eyes.
An oasis of light, oxygen light
fresh, salty, infinite, unspoken, untested

circular, smooth-edged, bearing down
rough, fragmented, grasping at your edge,
the finishing taste of salt.

It would have to be
so much more than this,
squinting as the wave

slams us over and under
the only solid ground
you (I) have left.

The Wind is Music

for Stephanie and Emily

A delicate hand put me down
by the sea.
Stephanie said,

*"Emily fell asleep on my chest.
I was in the rocking chair.
I had my Kindle next to me, read
for half an hour to make sure
she was in a deep sleep
before moving her."*

In Venice there is a dividing line between
the Grand Canal and all other canals.
When I hear your voice through the wall
it puts me at ease.

Walking on boards in San Marco Square
to get above the flooding, we pass
St. Mark's Basilica. Before they put the boards up
we bought two small watercolors
from an artist painting in the square.

At Harry's Bar
waiting for the sink water to get hot
I let it flow over my hands.
Looking out the window of your childhood bedroom

a lightness washes over me.
In early morning
a cleansing rain comes down
deep, spiritual. The wind is music.

Sky Flashed with Light

The beginning of the end starts with lunch.
Ghosts of lovers past join us.
Not everything always works out for everyone.

At 4:30 in the morning, stars out, crystal cold clear air
riding in a balloon over Albuquerque.
Fifty go up, forty-nine come down in one piece.

It's a spiritual thing, this falling in love
and out of the sky. No one to help
as it descends into electrical wires.

Sky flashed with light. Dinner is calm.
No strange faces intrude.
The balloon has been taken away, bodies removed.
It was a nine-day festival.

Northern Hotel

Wind
clatters against the side
of the house.

In the hills behind
the noise of the wind,
crickets and grasshopper

float in the air.
Doors close, lights flicker
even as you,

or someone like you,
shuts every exit.
Car doors slam.

Everyone fights to get
into the Northern Hotel.
Doors open. Guests

pile out back to look
at the Northern Lights arranged.
Across the horizon, against the wind
your arms cross
as if to say, *stop here*
wait until all this passes.

A Light Wind

Every time I pass your house
I go deeper into myself until
finally I see all the rooms empty,

my music gone, my books.
Art that once lined the wall, not there.
The moon floats above treeless branches.

The moon has broken off
a thousand little moons, each piece
a reflection of your eyes.

In our deepest soul we know
there are no pursuits of the flesh
after this.

Sometimes, we forget and think
Time Square's bright neon
will last forever.

Across the sky millions of blue stars.
In the morning, years of silence.
A light wind. Someone has passed.

A Previous Life

Morning is when I am awake and there is a dawn in me - Thoreau

And when
it all has
ended,

endlessly,
everywhere
and for

everyone
and only
unpolished

stone
roads remain,
roads

leading
to the blood
white face

of our moon,
an early moon,
blood roads.

Fear nothing
as the earth
returns

to its natural
form.
Each

and every star
returns
to its natural
astral body.

The Northern Lights
are speaking.
Dark moons flash.

The astral love
blue flowers.
The Big Dipper is everywhere.

Blue Jupiter,
blue ice,
gold

the color of falling,
blue
the color of crystals,

gold
the fool's color,
distant gold.

The dance of sea mist
on the moon
is calm.

All this is natural
and could not be
otherwise.

The Simple Changes

Only the mountains last
and small animals survive.
The simple change.

Sun sucks up water.
Sandstone shifts and dries.
Wind blows,

pushing water
away from the sea.
Mountains catch it.

The east coast was once oak,
great forests of oak.
The land was higher.

But the winds stopped
and trees died.
Tremendous heat cracked open the earth.

Many animals moved west
away from the sea.
Many died.

Masses of ice formed
and attracted the herds
into their light.

They began to eat seeds,
to use stars
to move slowly.

For years they moved slowly,
with no memory of the old.
More than once, everything vanished.

November

The darkness of night
comes early,

roaring winds
down
a cold canyon wall,

the softness of night
s quiet solitude.

The special warmth of sleeping
through it all, sheltered,
protected by the dawn.

Soft silent breathing.
Future hope
tempered with steel.

Sorrow
supported by pillars.

Fall

This fall
I wake early, lighter,
certain that the leaves remain,
sure of the strength I feel.
Two deer at the grass edge.

Falling brush and bare ground
blackened by the rain.
I open myself to no one.
Deer are everywhere,
black snakes and garden
cut across cracked land.

This fall
my eyes burn more
and my hands are colder.
Do not touch them or
I will take your heart,
and your soul will fly
out of your head and never return.

Balance

The sound of light falling away
leaves the air shaking
and leaves welcoming their end.

In this stillness
no one breathes that does not have to.
No one speaks.

The sun leaves a darkness
to cover the night.
Silence remains around us.

The wind blows slower
and brings less light
to the trees.

The wind is old and weak
and grows even older
and speaks less.

There is no blaming the wind.
It hardly moves,
except to brush the ground.

There is no blame,
only dancing,
in and out of your soul.

After the song
and the dancing are over
it will all be different.

A thunder will speak
and the sun will lift its head
as it flies away.

Water

It is after midnight.
Inside the earth
small animals are breathing

like fish in a mist sea.
Bits of eyes are floating.
I am dressed in reds and yellows.

There are webs of color
which are like black birds.
Rainbows form the skin of the sky.

Everyone is dancing,
drinking cold smoke,
eating the center of fruit.

Our seeds are stillborn
shaped into ovals or almost circles,
they are like lakes

reflecting my own face.
Taking your hands,
I taste the wild water and swallow.

Water flows along every edge.
Reeds float by, tossed
like a great cloud of broken rain.

Look into my eyes,
your own eyes are water.

Just Someone I Used to Know
life in balance

One day read some of these.
Know who I am. Know who you are.
The connection is everything.

Taos hot springs, Stavanger Fjord,
a Scotsman named Michael drinking Balvenie.
A young Spanish girl making a U-turn

running me off the road. These
are the peaceful moments before
cancer hits, breasts are cut off, lives change.

The connection is everything.
Spirit matter soars. Synapse of space and time.
The gap between then and now.

The old brick house showed its age. Crumbling
mortar, cracks near the windows, patched concrete.
Rickety stairs lead inside.

You lived upstairs and sometimes at night
I would see you looking out the window. The noise
of the trucks and ambulance always

bothered you. One night looking out you said,
"don't be afraid, you can go in me."
Now steam rises

off my coffee. Today
the front of our house is stone.
Cars drive by. Boys play basketball.

But the back is still untamed trees, branches
down, a dirt and sod space
inhabited by Snuffy, my tortoise.

The Morning Star

Here you see the Morning Star.
Who sees the Morning Star shall see more,
for he shall be wise.
                 - Black Elk, Oglala Sioux

It is early
and the night shakes
above the earth.

Pine needles
and cat o' nine tails
are flat black.

The few clouds are puffs.
Woods awake
in flashes.

Yellows and greens
reflect in the bark.
Faces appear

in the flowers. Tiny faces
appear in the flowers.
Faceless

angels shroud the bark.
Light begins to disappear,
completely.

The sound of shaking
leaves break the stillness.
Cold air slips

between branches.
The Morning Star is out
and begins to open.

Beyond the faded sky
clouds drift past the trees.

Closer to God

Shoes got by devilish ways will burn your feet.
            - Langston Hughes

WARNING – *This poem contains strong language.*

There are things that people do not like to hear.
There are things that people do not like to say.
So many people criticize so many people.

Sometimes I question my own life.
Martin Luther King Jr. questioned all of our lives.
He asked us to be the people we could be.

Everyone has suffered loss in their lives.
Everyone has suffered injustice.
Everyone grieves for different things.

Some of us can rise above the grief.
Leaves turn red and rust on oak and elm.
White flakes line my window.

I think of afternoons at the cemetery standing
near my son. Thirty years and three days.
Martin was thirty-nine years and almost three months.

We lean on each other's shoulders.
We carry on where he left off.
Blessed is the memory of Dr. Martin Luther King, Jr.

Blessed is the memory of all we lost.
May his soul always soar above us and guide us
on the path of justice for all.

Langston Hughes said,
My soul has grown deep like the rivers.
Martin's soul was deep like the rivers
and still is.

Living Beyond My Means

Above the clouds I feel the change.
Heaven's gate swings back again.
I had a glimpse of love and death,
so much life, all the breadth.

A fool's journey never ends
between forest and sea
something more than friends.

Sun burning holes in my eyes
an opening to wider skies.
Both feet firmly planted on the ground
I live beyond my means, iron bound.

The Chamber of Light

Dec. 21, 1976. First day of winter.
22 degrees, wind
gusting to 50. Wind chill 15 below.

Looking at the earth from the eye
of an eagle, an occasional black speck,
jackrabbit, prairie dog, vole.

All the talismans I keep—
feather, smooth stones, dry branches
are invisible.

Red tile roofs above.
Tranquil moments cannot last.
Yes, the sea is still there

only harder to find.
No, all does not always go well.
The essence of life is karma.

About the Author

Stuart P. Radowitz has taught English, English language arts, critical reading, and creative writing in the Uniondale School District (Long Island), Nassau BOCES Teenage Parenting Program (TAP), and New York City Public Schools, as well as Molloy University and Farmingdale State College, SUNY.

As an undergraduate at Syracuse University, where he won the Whiffen Prize in Poetry, he studied with Stephen Dunn, Donald Justice, and W.D. Snodgrass. At Colorado State University, he received his master's degree in creative writing, workshopping with Mary Crow, Stanley Plumly, and Bill Tremblay.

Stuart's poems have appeared in many journals and reviews, including the following anthologies: *64 Best Poets of 2018* (Black Mountain Press); *Long Island Sounds: 2023 An Anthology of Poetry From Maspeth to Montauk and Beyond* (The North Sea Poetry Scene Press); *NYC from the Inside: NYC Through the Eyes of the Poets Who Live Here* (Blue Light Press); *Pandemic Puzzle Poems* (Blue Light Press); *Paumanok Transition* (Island Sound Press); *Poets to Come: A Poetry Anthology* (Local Gems Press); and *Poets Speaking to Poets: Echoes and Tributes* (Ars Omnia Press).

His first book of poetry, *Snow Hangs on the Branches of Evergreens*, was published by Blue Light Press in 2020, a pandemic book baby.

He lives on Long Island with his wife Sherry, Violet the cat, Mr. T. the hybrid aquatic turtle, and Snuffy, his giant sixty-pound tortoise. His daughter Stephanie, her husband Dave, granddaughter Emily, and grandson Ryan live in Connecticut.

Stuart is grateful for every poem and hopes that each tells a story.

www.ingramcontent.com/pod-product-compliance
Lightning Source LLC
Chambersburg PA
CBHW031205160426
43193CB00008B/513